Praise for "D

"Trust in him at all times... (Psalm 62:8). Just as the Psalms are known for expressing the full range of human emotions, so 'Dear God... Really?' expresses the highs and lows of one man's stumbling pursuit of the God he trusts, but doesn't always understand. The prayers are honest, angry, witty, convicting and thought-provoking. I recommend it. Thanks for sharing, Bryan"

—**Jimmy Davis** Pastor, Carrollton, TX

"Dude... I love the book. I love that kind of raw honesty. You said things I believe we have all thought a dozen times or more but a few of us have the guts to say it and pray it. I think it will be a great help to many people."

— **Donald Gibson** Pastor, Freeport, TX

"Bryan has created entertaining examples of honest dialog, crucial to any recovery process. He brings humor to the hard to deal with feelings we all have. 'Dear God... Really?' is a not so subtle inspiration to others to speak the truth to themselves. This book of prayers has gone over very well with our clients in recovery."

— **Dr. Charles Graham** Program Director for Celebrate Recovery at Sober Living By The Sea

"'Dear God... Really?' is an incredible book that I will want to share with as many of my friends as possible. I will look forward to the release and buying a bunch of copies as gifts."

— **Larry J. Sundquist** President of Sundquist Homes

"These prayers are about as honest as you can get. We've all said at one time or another, "When I get to Heaven, I want to ask God..."? Bryan has probably asked your question here, and he's done it in a way that will make you laugh. It's okay to ask God the hard questions, and it's okay for our prayers not to sound very religious. God gets it. I can't wait to hear His answers!"

— **Steve Webb** Host of the Lifespring!, LifespringMedia.com

From the Web...

"I got my preview and read the whole thing today. Love it! Honest, irreverent, poignant, and REAL. Thanks for sharing."

—Julie Christiansen

"Enjoyed the book! Love the humor but love the transparency more! Thanks for keeping it real..."

— Darryl Matson

"Bryan's new book is the reason he's my friend. He's not afraid to share. Love it."

— Tim Driver

"I'm SO in love with your pragmatism, honesty & humor in 'Dear God… Really?'"

— Lydia Deitrich

"A humorous and sometimes irreverent way of looking at everyday experiences, yet teaching a lesson."

— Bryan Buchaolz

"Takes everyday questions to God, the way Grandma did not teach us. Thought provoking and entertaining. It is speaking to me during a time that I really need it."

— Bill Ricks

"I can't come up with a comical review. It's too funny on its own!"

— Billy Kellum

"I want more—time to write your next one now."

— Leesa Munger

Follow Bryan!

facebook.com/BryanSoulManDuncan

twitter.com/Bryan_Duncan

bryanduncan.com

Dear God... REALLY?

Prayers You Won't Hear in Church

By Bryan Duncan

www.deargodreally.com

Engage Faith Press • Seattle, WA

An *Original* Publication of Engage Faith Press
PO Box 2222, Poulsbo WA 98370

www.engagefaith.com

First Engage Faith trade paperback printing February 2010
10 9 8 7 6 5 4 3 2 1

ISBN 978-0-9841658-1-0

Photography by Lynnette Siler
Printed in the U.S.A.

ENGAGE
FAITH
PRESS

This book is dedicated to my grandmother, Anna Forney

At 78 years old, Anna could still put her sons and grandsons on their knees in a "lock fingers" wrestling match. She grew up on a ranch in Kansas in the worst of the Great Depression. She was still mowing her own lawn at eighty. She told us stories of racing horses and killing rattlesnakes with a two-by-four as a kid.

Today the sound of crickets at night still reminds me of Grandma's house, where I would sleep on the screened-in front porch. Her place was the family Mecca to be returned to every summer. Charlie was her husband and a railroad engineer for the Denver and Rio Grande Western. He had a special train whistle signal just to let her know he was coming home. You could hear it across the Grand Junction valley.

Anna was a believer—prayed some of my earliest prayers with me. She prayed for everybody all the time. I'm convinced the Denver Broncos won the Super Bowl as a direct result of her relationship with God. She liked 'em 'cause the quarterback looked like one of her grandsons.

Her "mission field" was 1 husband, 2 sons, 4 daughters, 35 grandchildren, 67 great-grandchildren and 29 great-great-grandchildren. She never missed a kid's birthday in 60 years. She died February 21st, 2005 at age 97, and most of her descendants are in some form of ministry.

Dear God… I miss her desperately. Hug her for all of us… but don't get in a "lock fingers" wrestling match with her!

Dear God... REALLY?

Prayers You Won't
Hear in Church

Dear God...

Dear God...

Dear God...

Introduction

The one thing that all faiths have in common is the presence of reasonable doubt!

Combine that with poorly-educated assumptions, opinions, personal preference, complaints and questions, and you have the makings of the kind of prayers that only God could tolerate and the rest of us just laugh at. There is a little bit of the antagonist in us all. And if God himself were to stick his head through the clouds to show his face to the world, we would still never agree on what we saw. Most of us have seen at least portions of "God's Letter" to people, and we can't agree on what he said. This book is a collection of prayers: what I really wanted to say before I edited them to make me appear more spiritual.

I was born in the West and raised in the South. My dad was a Pentecostal preacher and a traveling evangelist in my early years. I sat through more sermons in a month than some people attend in a lifetime. As a kid, I was known to sing the church hymns on purpose in the relative minor key while those around me sang the correct melody. They thought I just couldn't sing very well. Thing is, I was bored easily. Which is quite a feat, given the fervent and fiery kind of services small Pentecostal churches have. My religion was born of obligation—seeing how it was the only world I was aware of in the beginning.

But as my career as a Christian Singer gained international status, I found myself in all kinds of church services. I was singing for ministries with all sorts of agendas. But "fitting in" became a problem for me. There were unspoken rules of behavior, always varied and sometimes conflicting. It was no wonder that I found myself thoroughly discontent after thirty years of "compliance." It never meant that I threw the baby (Jesus) out with the bathwater, but I certainly had to wrap him in a towel and clean out the tub. There is an inescapable fatigue living in plain sight of someone else's faith. And in my early 40's, I discovered I needed to settle on my own.

Around the beginning of my rehabilitation, something really struck me. In step 11 of the 12 steps of recovery, I read: "We sought to improve our conscious contact with God as we understand him." This put a different spin on the idea of devotion and meditation for me. "Improve my conscious contact." Start from scratch and introduce yourself! I was asked by a therapist to write a letter to God as a way of dealing with my hurts, anger and resentments. I rolled my eyes at the assignment, but upon writing the words, "Dear God," I was given a freedom to say anything I wanted! It would become the beginning of a wonderful relief. What I didn't expect, however, was a relationship, finally, with an unbiased friend who could put up with anything I could possibly dish out. And I began to find a way back to a faith I'd always known.

My prayers are mostly an "exorcism" of my own self-centeredness these days… with the occasional glimmer of a pure heart. I can only laugh at my faulty assumptions before I even open my mouth to a truly all-knowing being. My answers to prayer come usually in the form of a change in my own perception.

Even here my prayers are edited, mostly for a humorous take on real struggles. In these pages, you will find much sarcasm. But insight begins with an acknowledgement of ignorance. I've found that reading my own prayers is like a golfer watching himself on camera as he swings the club at the ball. Suddenly, you know why the ball isn't being directed where you'd like.

My prayers have been haphazard for most of my life. Because they were always last-minute, desperate cries of need. Had I started with the honesty of my own feelings, I might have found a stronger connection, and my prayers might have been better directed. I get better help from those I have a deeper relationship with. The same is true of a connection with God.

This book is a collection of prayers: what I really wanted to say before I edited my own feelings out in hopes of receiving a better response.

— Bryan Duncan

Dear God... You Sound Too Good To Be True

Excuse me for being nervous here, but upon reading the New Testament side of the Bible, Jesus seems to be the perfect answer for everybody's problem. I've been taught that if it sounds too good to be true, it's probably not true. So, let me see if I've got this right: I believe. I'm forgiven. I don't have to fear. And I get to live forever in a mansion just over the hilltop, where there's no more pain! Sounds like a sales pitch to me, where's the catch?

It says in Article 4, paragraph 3, and line 16 of your bylaws that you let Jesus serve my death sentence. I've always believed in capital punishment, unless, of course, I was the guilty party. But I wasn't even aware that I was on trial in this case. Thanks for the bailout. Grace is a wonderful thing.

But I'm feeling a little more than obligated at this point. Your story makes my free will seem to be a real waste of my time. In reading the fine print in your contract, I owe you big time. How do I repay this debt out of a right motive when obligation is obvious? Forgive me for my cynicism here, but I bought some Health Insurance recently. The language was pretty close to your own, and I'm still paying for that. I guess I'm having trouble trusting your "verbiage" because of the people you've created "in your image."

Thanks for lettin' me share... Amen.

Dear God... Do You Believe In Atheists?

Met a waitress today, said she didn't believe in you. So I guess she's free on Christmas. It wasn't just that she didn't believe in you, though. It was like she was really pissed that you aren't there! I wondered if you'd missed her birthday. She looked really tired, too. "When you die, that's it," she says. So here she is slaving away at this little nickel-a-day job. I wondered what kind of bigger picture she might see for doing all the little stuff on a daily basis?

I don't exactly have a picture of you in my wallet either, I told her. I'm just kinda trusting that yer getting my emails. I got no real proof. But I have lived through some really interesting coincidences. I was told that this is your way of remaining anonymous. Now why would you wanna do that? This is exactly why people don't think yer there! Sometimes I think you like to play a little game of hide-and-seek. But a lot of people just aren't in the mood.

Personally, I think she might have been stepped on one-too-many times. Doesn't seem like she's havin' a lot of fun running her own life. But here is where I think you are really there, 'cause I'm wanting to give her a thirty percent tip. I know that's not me! I think you are pushing me into doing it. Lord, I don't have the extra money to start paying off all the angry, hopeless people in the world. Anyway, I sure hope you exist, 'cause now it looks like I'm just talking to myself.

Thanks for lettin' me share... Amen.

Dear God... I Don't Like Some Of Your Friends

Do you have a list I could see of people you've endorsed? I find it annoying that the barely-self-aware seem to have all the answers for me. I'd get a second opinion, but "God People" seem to regurgitate the same Scriptures like they're handing out free prescriptions of dopamine. I know in the Olden Days you spoke through prophets who dressed funny for the times. I'm assuming Moses walked into Pharaoh's court looking like a homeless guy, initially written off as an escapee from the Desert Center for the Mentally Ill-Prepared.

These days, it's hard to tell who your "Reps" are. Soon as someone starts throwing Scriptures and God-talk, I'm immediately suspicious. And I'm afraid to stand next to 'em 'cause it'll make me look bad. I don't mind speaking up to defend you or confessing to non-believers that you are my friend. But do I have to add a bumper sticker and a sense of "other world" insanity to speak of some sort of spiritual depth? Scripture-quoters always bring a smug fix before they've heard the problem. Why aren't you embarrassed? Looks like poor marketing from my perspective. Anyway, I suppose it makes me feel better if I can point out the defects of character in others. I was wondering if that could be my "ministry." I have a natural inclination already. But first, I'd like to take up an offering.

Thanks for lettin' me share... Amen.

Dear God...
I'll Take It From Here

Thanks for the jump start. I'm O.K. now. Besides, I have an "accountability partner" who's gonna look in on me from time to time. If I run into any trouble, I got his cell number. So that's one less thing for you to worry about. That thirty days I spent in Lunatics Anonymous—for people with more than one problem—was just what I needed. I'm back on my feet, though. I'm good. I haven't done anything really wrong in about two weeks. I read those 12 steps in about two days! My life was unmanageable there for a minute, but now that I've acknowledged you and turned over my will a couple times, I'm feeling pretty confident that I can get back into the swing. That shrink gave me enough medication to cover the blackouts and the seizures for a while. And with the Prozac, I haven't been depressed, either. My friends are all sayin' how much I've changed. Hey, I'm getting along with everybody, too. We finished step 12 last night in my support group. I got a gold coin to take with me. So I guess I'm off.

It was great hangin' with ya, though. I am gonna pay you back real soon, too, 'cause I just appreciate what you've done for me.

Listen, lets keep in touch. I mean it. We'll get together around Christmas, just me and you. Talk about old times. It'll be great.

Thanks for lettin' me share... Amen.

Dear God... I'm Back

Don't know what happened out there. I was just minding my own business. You know, toeing the line and everything. Trying to be a good person. Trouble just found me, what can I say? I wouldn't have a problem if it weren't for all the people I run into. It's their fault I ended up where I am. I was just trying to cope with their unreasonable expectations! And their behaviors! What in your name is up with that? People are just weird. Mostly 'cause they're not at all like me. They think they can just lie, cheat and steal anytime they feel like it. I, on the other hand, was just trying to get my needs met. I mean, where's the benevolence here? This world is so screwed up. I'm sure grateful you made hell for people like that!

Sorry I have to keep coming back, but I'm not in a good place this week. Everything keeps unraveling; I can't seem to make people do what I want. They don't listen to me. I was wondering if you could slap some sense into 'em. Ungodly lowlifes, the whole bunch of 'em! They're selfish and self-centered, controlling, manipulating... and that's just my living relatives! Why on earth would anyone wanna conjure up the dead?! Like we don't have enough stupid opinions and bad information from the pie-holes that are still breathing.

I've been told that these are your creations, by the way. What on earth were you thinking? I'm beginning to believe that the third rock from the sun is really just the trash can for stuff that didn't turn out the way you wanted. I understand the creative process myself. There's always a rough draft, and you kind of work it as you go. That's why I'm back: I need some creative adjustments. I'm not playing well with others!

What were the names of those three guys in the "fiery furnace" that people tried to cremate while they were still alive? "Sad Sack, Horshack and Offend-Me-Mo"? Everyone was astonished that they weren't burning in the flames. I'm not in a literal furnace here, but I can smell my hair on fire. Just from the little digs people say to me, I smell like a smoldering bicycle tire. I'm at least getting singed around the edges. I'm wondering if you could give me a fresh coat of fire retardant.

Thanks for lettin' me share… Amen.

Dear God...
Make Me A Success

I'm not sure what that means, really, but my vision is to be independently wealthy, so I don't need anybody. I'll pay appropriate homage to you, of course, and act humble. I'll give to those in need, too, I just don't want to be one of them. I'd like to be in control and look good to everyone around me.

I don't know if you've noticed, but I do look a lot more spiritual when I'm not lacking anything. It's easier to tell others about you and how you made it all happen. It's a win-win for both of us. As I see it, nobody listens to poor people! Here's where your plan for spreading the Gospel might not be working. Most of your followers have very little influence in their communities. The Gospel is the "Good News" right? So what could be better than not being needy?

Thanks for lettin' me share... Amen.

Dear God...
I'd Like To Delegate

Every good leader has "people." You know, to handle all the little details of running a bigger picture. I'm getting bogged down in the small stuff, handling it myself. Maybe you could appoint a couple more angels to run the maintenance on my pride and attitude.

These things are messing up my relationship with the people I'm trying to help. My awareness of their needs is starting to suffer. I'm not effecting the kind of change in the lives of others that I know you'd like to see.

Thanks for lettin' me share... Amen.

Dear God...
Who Do I Trust?

I don't see anywhere in your book where you ask me to trust anyone but you. But I'm finding a lot of situations where I have to choose to believe someone. I watched two of your "spokesmen" on TV the other day—they had completely different points of view about who you are and what your will is.

Though both of them seemed to know exactly what you had in mind for me. It was more than you've said to me personally! Are you talking to them about me? I'd really like to be in the loop on these discussions 'cause I'm getting a lot of feedback second-hand.

I hear, "I love you," from time to time from people who say they love you. Usually they are not familiar with my behaviors, though. It's starting to feel like an opening line for another agenda. Guys in shirts and ties ridin' bicycles, folks dressed to the nines offering me free literature expounding on the real truth. Church people! Very untrusting of my experiences, never much interested, either.

Answering with Scripture in a dogmatic tone, opposing every feeling I have. I mentioned to a couple the other day that I just finished talking with you. They acted like I was nuts. They left in a rather quick fashion after that. Hope you don't mind if I drop your name to get away from people I don't trust.

Thanks for lettin' me share... Amen.

Dear God... What's It Like Being Omniscient?

It must be nice to know everything before it happens. Or is that just plain boring? I wondered if you miss the surprises. I kinda like discovering things I didn't know before. Better yet, I love knowing stuff I didn't know I knew once. When I was younger I was one of those who knew it all. I think I just forgot a lot of it. But then, a lot of what I knew doesn't apply anymore because everything has changed. I should have known that would happen.

I gotta say, I'd make better friends if I knew the outcome before next year, though. I have some acquaintances that think they know everything. And they are just plain irritating. Maybe it's because I know just enough to know that they don't really know.

You must have a completely different sense of adventure, knowing everything before it happens. I don't know how that works, to know before you decide. I talk to people who know something better than I do before I make decisions—counselors, consultants—but you can't hold them responsible for what they don't know.

I'm happy to trust you, knowing that you know what I don't. At least I don't have to explain everything to people who want to know. But what I'd really like to understand is why I make poor decisions, knowing full well that they are.

Thanks for lettin' me share... Amen.

Dear God... Do You Take Out The Trash?

What do you mean, "take all my thoughts captive"? Currently, my mind is holding me hostage. You're using a lot of battlefield scenarios when you talk. So why do I have this mental picture of pinning moths to a poster board? I'm not really sure I wanna start an insect collection. I haven't taken my thoughts too seriously. My mind is a miniature version of a super-collider. Have you seen the clutter in my head? My whole house is a mess, and you're asking me to organize my closet.

I'm trying to say all the right things out in the open to come off as the positive person people like to see. So where do I put all those negative thoughts? I've been stockpiling them in my head. It's a virtual trash compactor in there. I heard a chef say that every kitchen has to have a set of mixing bowls. I'm currently using one old coffee can. I've got all the ingredients in one giant bowl. Trouble is, I'm using more than one recipe, and what I get is an awful-tasting Jell-o stew.

I've been told I have the ability to compartmentalize. But that's how I developed my split personalities. My mental kitchen isn't laid out right. My garbage disposal is in the refrigerator. So where do I put the dumpster? Do you have a herd of swine that I could cast my thoughts into? It seems a little demeaning to ask you to take out the trash. But I'm a basket-case, and I'm all out of liners.

Thanks for lettin' me share... Amen.

Dear God... When Can It Be About Me?

Everybody seems to be in a hell-fired hurry for me to be humble and see a bigger picture. I'm afraid to brush my teeth because I might be too focused on myself. I got a friend who just finished reading that *Purpose Driven Life* book. I guess it's about serving others, mostly.

But he's expecting me to volunteer all my time for free because "it's not about you." I'm getting a little tired of hearing that. It feels like I don't really matter, like I'm supposed to just be invisible.

I keep hearing from the pulpit how special I am 'cause you love me. And how you've given me a power to go out and really shine. But then they turn around and talk about how wretched I am for being self-centered and selfish. I'm getting a little confused. What is it? Am I valuable or worthless?

I feel like my service to others is being manipulated sometimes for the "purpose" of someone else's 401K! It seems like there should be a balance of give-and-take in a relationship. How do I give if I don't have anything in supply? Honestly, it feels like I've driven my "purpose" out of gas.

Thanks for lettin' me share... Amen.

Dear God... My Forgiveness Isn't Working!

I forgave someone a few months ago. You remember her? Well, right when I think I've moved on, I have these replays of her outrageous transgressions against me. Is that like an "aftershock" or something? Did I not forgive her right? It feels like I buried a cat that isn't quite dead yet. First of all, that woman is still alive and well. Just seeing her sometimes reminds me of what I forgave her for!

I've heard that you "don't remember" transgressions once you've been asked for forgiveness. But with all due respect, it seems like a "God-assisted" ability.

I, on the other hand, am not you! I can't seem to "forget" when people hurt me. As I recall in Scripture, you had to kill somebody for the sins committed against you, and your own son volunteered! I can't get my son to even call me back. Plus, they tell me I don't get to kill anybody now because of the price your son has already paid for transgressions.

Right now, I'm feeling a lack of satisfaction in knowing a price was already exacted. I guess I'm just seeing the damage done to my trust of others, whether forgiveness is offered or not. I have no problem forgetting appointments or anniversaries or where I put my car keys. Maybe you could transfer some of that memory loss to the things that really hurt!

Thanks for lettin' me share... Amen.

Dear God... I'm Clean, Right?

Let me get this straight. I confess to you, and you "wash" my sins away? I seem to be getting dirty again in the spin cycle. My washing machine at home has an "agitation" device. Is that part of your cleansing process for failures? Is there a time element that I'm missing?

I feel like maybe I need to soak longer 'cause the stains aren't coming out. And by the way, I'm fading with the repetition of cleanings! It doesn't appear that I'm "wash and wear" material. Is there a delicate cycle for this kind of cleansing? Or do you just wash sins out the old-fashioned way: down by the river, pounding 'em out on a rock?

When I put on clean clothes after a hot shower, I feel noticeably better for a few hours. I wondered if you have better feelings about me for a while when I'm clean.

Purity doesn't seem to be completely possible down here. My white socks never look like they did when I bought 'em. And when I wear white, it's almost guaranteed that I will spill the mustard front-and-center, where everyone will see it. I think I'd prefer a "saintly robe" in a paisley print so my sins would be less visible, at least.

Thanks for lettin' me share... Amen.

Dear God... Are You On Speakerphone?

I've gotten pretty comfortable telling you my sins. I'm still alive; I guess that's a good sign. But it's heightened my own awareness of my discrepancies.

We're not on speakerphone, are we? 'Cause I'm feeling like people know stuff I didn't tell them. When they don't call me back, I start worrying that the rumor mill has been grinding me to pieces. Is that guilt or paranoia?

I heard that you give people the gift of discernment. I assume, at least in part, that's the ability to see through other people's false motives. So maybe you gave my friends a special ability to see through me. Well, now, that doesn't feel good.

I wondered, though, if maybe other people's guardian angels are passin' along stuff they overheard me say in your office. I get a lot of free judgment even when people don't know the exact nature of my sins.

I think I might have liked denial better. At least I wasn't self-conscious. I try to make insecurity look like humility. If I'm quiet, maybe people will assume I'm humble. I noticed that when I'm not talking or doing anything, I tend to look more spiritual. Can that work for now?

Thanks for lettin' me share... Amen.

Dear God... I Need You To Kill Someone!

You know who the problem is. I know you probably won't do this for me. But could you at least allow them to NOT prosper? I don't see an ounce of suffering in their direction. And after all they've done! It's not just me. They're hurting a lot of people. I think it would be better for the community as a whole if this person were at least allowed to have a catastrophic accident that would render them unable to speak!

Maybe you could just give them a mild stroke or something. It might keep them from being all up in everybody's business. I've decided: they can't hear you at all and have no intention of changing directions even a little bit. I'd like to lay hands on 'em. Put a pencil in their ear, and drive it all the way through. There seems to be a clog; nothing is reaching their brain.

Why do I have to change if they don't? I guess that's the real question. It just really bugs me that not only are they getting away with stuff that I can't, but it seems to be working for them! Where's the justice?

Thanks for lettin' me share… Amen.

Dear God...
Can We Tweet?

I was hoping you would accept me as a friend on Facebook, but I haven't been confirmed. How about me following you on Twitter? If you could just tell me in a 140 words what yer doing right now, maybe I'd stop bothering you.

I don't get a response from my kids unless I text, so yer not the only one who won't pick up the phone and talk to me directly. I'm sure I'd be filling up yer page, though. Every two minutes. I'm so annoying, I've even stopped talking to myself! I don't listen to what I'm saying. I can't even remember what I asked you for. By the time I get a message back from you, I forgot what we were talking about!

But Twitter is the new social media response system we use so we can all sit in isolation and chat with people who aren't in the room. Or ignore the people who actually are. They probably won't be listening to you, either, if you ramble on. But short bursts of insight might get you a "ReTweet." Yer message could be instantly broadcast all over the place! You really should look into the new media as a way to communicate. I'm just saying that someone like you would probably have a ton of followers!

I hate to tell you this, but if you are waiting for people to have a free moment to talk to you, I think yer gonna lose a lot of followers. You gotta get in on the ground level with the new technology, and, hopefully, you'll have a greater impact in the long run. It's just a thought, mind you. Let me know if you need an idea for your ID and Password.

Thanks for lettin' me share... Amen.

Dear God...
Yer Not Following My Plan

I read somewhere that you know every motive in a man's heart. I didn't see the need for a memo on this. My intentions are good! So I was wondering why you haven't gotten back to me on my plans—they could really fix a lot of broken stuff!

No offense here, but your divine intervention seems a little slow. I'm worried that you, as an immortal, might have forgotten that I only have maybe seventy years to get things done. I'm falling behind. I could really use your help in moving my plans forward. I'll give you all the glory, of course.

Thanks for lettin' me share... Amen.

Dear God... You Fish?

Hi, it's me again. I came across a little miracle your son performed where he pulled money out of a fish's mouth to pay taxes! I had to read that twice to be sure I caught it. It's in there: chapter 17, book one of the "Jesus Years." It only mentions that he did that once. I haven't heard of anybody paying taxes by fishing since then, either. Is that still an option? 'Cause I need a miracle to pay my taxes.

It appears the entire amount pulled out of the fish went to pay the tax. Well, I see that hasn't changed in two thousand years. Did Peter get to keep the fish after reeling it in? King David mentions earlier in your book something about "Thy rod and thy staff shall comfort me..." I'm hoping it's a fly rod with a twenty-pound test line. Jesus told his fishermen friends on another occasion they would "net" more by fishing on the other side of the boat. I personally thought he was suggesting they switch occupations. The tax collectors are doing most of the fishing these days. Yeah, they call it an audit! But we both know they're just fishing. God forbid I pull a mackerel out of a pond teeming with minnows!

My problem is I'm getting taxed quarterly every year. I think I might need to land a blue whale to extract enough money to cover the king's ransom. Me? I'm fishing off the bow now... nothin'.

Thanks for lettin' me share... Amen.

Dear God...
People Keep Sinning!

I've told 'em to "just say no." Even when they see the damage they are doin', they don't stop. They might change their behavior, but that seems to just redefine the parameters of new sins! How many sins are there, by the way? Are they just the same seven sins in a new outfit?

Why is it that being good doesn't look good? It's a boring read in a movie script, I'm told. The best books have the most awful people in 'em. Do we like that because it makes us feel better about ourselves?

I tried to write a story about a guy that never did anything wrong. It was about a page long. No challenge, no redemption, no sad parts, no euphoric ending, and, most of all, no surprises. He lived happily ever after, but I didn't really wanna hear about it.

I think I'm seeing the point in the way you've set up the "greatest story ever told." Thanks for making a longer book.

Thanks for lettin' me share... Amen.

Dear God...
Not Now!

I'm requesting an extension on my benevolent service obligations. Loving my neighbor has become something of a quagmire recently. I hadn't counted on the incredible investment of time it might require. Nor did I expect the indifferent and sometimes obnoxious behavior from the recipients. And, currently, it is running a close second to "Death and Disability" in the way of inconvenience.

I understand that I should not expect any form of remuneration in these efforts, but, frankly, I'm disappointed in the lack of any reciprocation even in the way of personal attitude.

I would like to postpone further outreach until such a time as mutual contractual expectations might be realized. Please find the attached list of personal boundary violations I have incurred in recent months. I would greatly appreciate your perusal of these infractions and your granting me an immediate temporary dismissal of compassionate responsibility for my fellow man. I would also like to file a "Cease and Desist" order directed at those listed in the aforementioned attachment.

Thanks for lettin' me share... Amen.

Dear God... Whatever!

I read the "serenity prayer" again this morning. There's a line in there about praying ONLY for your will and the power to carry that out. I'm having trouble with the "your will" part. I get apathetic about prayer when I don't get to control the outcome. My prayers start to come out like, "Yeah... do what you want. I'm gonna go 'change the things I can.'"

I know from the beginning that's not a great attitude, but it still comes out that way. I'm thinking about how I've prayed for things recently, where you answered in such a different direction it didn't feel like it was attached to the same prayer. I suppose you knew what your will was going to be and how I should have phrased the request in the first place. Thanks for the edit!

I'm wondering, though, if you might work a miracle today with regard to my attitude about "your will." A bad attitude is like a headache. I can admit to it, but that doesn't make it go away. Honestly, I like 'my will' most of the time... and to ask ONLY for your will leaves me with a little bit of a pout. I feel like the preacher who's prayed for too many people in a day: exhausted, he says, "Dear God... Whatever!"

Forgive me for tryin' to answer my own prayers!

Thanks for lettin' me share... Amen.

Dear God... I'll Be Right Back

Listen, here's the thing, I got a few plans that I'm not sure yer gonna be proud of. But I need to handle this little problem that I'm having with that idiot I told you about.

I'm just gonna go give him a piece of my mind. I got this one. No need for you to be there, though. I'd let you handle it, but yer way too forgiving, and he is taking advantage of what I think is a little too much grace. I'm gonna go "minister" to him. He's a mean drunk, and when he starts spoutin' off about how faith in you is just a "crutch," the irony isn't lost on me.

I learned in rehab that I have to set reasonable boundaries with other people. But he doesn't seem to recognize mine, so I thought I'd just go teach him how to "turn his other cheek." If he sees how quickly he can "cross over Jordan," maybe he'll "see the light" just before the lights go out.

Thanks for lettin' me share... Amen.

Dear God...
Where's The Blessing?

I donated a pretty healthy sum of money to a Christian organization two weeks ago. And they haven't mentioned it to anyone else. I have also not seen any reciprocal blessing from your camp yet.

They told me you would bless me if I gave. I could really milk this in the way of a demonstration to others about how giving works. So I'm waiting for you to kick in yer half. I know you take ten percent off the top; I'm good with that. But I have exceeded your requirements in the way of remuneration.

I'm just waiting for the blessings they said would come my way. I normally give selflessly and anonymously, but that hasn't really paid off too well. Nobody seems to know where to return the favor.

I'm worried. The blessings aren't just in the way of good feelings about doing something charitable are they? That's a nice little perk, don't get me wrong, but feeling good has a way of dissipating even more rapidly than my bank account.

A lot of yer organizations talk about giving like it is a real financial investment that will pay bigger dividends than I've actually seen. Buildings and property are built and purchased "for the moving forward of the ministry," but I'm not really sure who's on the deed. Do you hold the Titles to the land and facilities? I'm sorry about being a little suspicious, but I feel like somebody's making a buck or two off of you.

Thanks for lettin' me share… Amen.

Dear God... Just Checkin'

I asked one of your "servants" for a big favor a while back. He said, "I'll pray about it." I wondered if you had heard from him. It's been several weeks. I got the impression that he wasn't all that excited about helping me to begin with. But he did say he was gonna check with you. I'm sure you have some rules on confidentiality, but maybe you could just give me some kind of nod that he even speaks to you. Yes or no? I don't think I was on his short list of things to talk to you about.

I'm inclined to think that he was just blowing me off. But why does he have to make you the reason he's uncooperative? I don't see the point in all that. Just makes me think that he thinks I don't know you at all. Like I gotta wait for him to ask you what you might do for me! You seem to be an easy mark to be used for some people's over-inflated sense of self worth.

He reminds me of that guy from the IRS who lives down the street from me: carries this grand sense of power, the little man standing behind the big curtain. I call him Mr. Wizard. It's just kinda irritating that Mr. "I'll Pray About It" is hangin' in my same circle of God-friends, and we're still getting conflicting memos from the head office. Someone is obviously jamming your transmissions. So here I am prayin' about him prayin' about me. Seems like spiritual bureaucracy. No wonder nothin's getting done.

That guy asked me how I was doin' the other day. "I don't know," I told him, "a friend of mine is still prayin' about it."

Thanks for lettin' me share... Amen.

Dear God... Everybody's Busy!

Everywhere I go, I have to take a number to be heard. I call, get a recording, and spend fifteen minutes playing with the phone keys on my cell. And then I hear how wonderful it is to visit their "easy-to-use" website.

That comes with an application for a password and an ID number, usually. I have to have an appointment to talk to anybody. I got an invoice for a conversation I had yesterday! He called it a "consultation fee." I was standing in line with him at the bank! I asked him which line was actually moving.

By the way, you're not charging me for this conversation are you? I'm just looking for a little free empathy.

I have a support group that's free, but I only get three to five minutes to share. Just giving my name and my problem takes up most of that! I do have a good working relationship with several answering machines, though. I'm not getting much insight, but I've become very comfortable with playing back what I just heard myself say. And, yes, I am happy with the message I just left! But what I'd really like is a response.

Thanks for lettin' me share… Amen.

Dear God... Can I Be Humble If I Look Good Doin' It?

I saw a picture of an evangelist in a real shiny suit kneeling carefully to embrace a 'poor, starving child.' She was disheveled, and he had every hair in place. It was a pitch for me to send money to him for her! I wouldn't take a picture like that.

But I know I still want to look like a saint when I do something noteworthy and selfless at the same time. Probably doesn't happen too often. So let's get a picture. I'd like to have my name in large print, too, when the credits roll on the footage!

Does that really count? Can I look good being humble? I gotta tell you, it's a real effort to do something anonymously. 'Cause my close friends don't see how wonderful I can be most of the time. I really need a little "visible humility" to balance the scales in my favor. This is my humble prayer, dear Lord, just let others see how sacrificial I'm being... Hello? God? Are you still there?... How come yer not saying anything?

Thanks for lettin' me share... Amen.

Dear God... Wait Just A Minute

I just had a birthday in the month of March. I'm 56! I was looking at the calendar yesterday, and it dawned on me that last year in February I was actually 54! Two years younger than I am now! I'm feeling a little ripped off. As if my life isn't going by fast enough already, I have to claim two years of age difference in just 13 months!

This feels like the fine print in a contract where I discover the "hidden fees." And the fees are ALWAYS "applicable." "Participation" will vary, too, and "qualifications" and "requirements" for the "free" anything manage to weed out everybody.

I'm not askin' to live forever here, by the way. I'd like to die before I've forgotten my own name and after my bank accounts are empty. I'm spending my money about as fast as I'm aging, what with all the extra medications and body part replacements coming in my future. Those little "procedures" in the doctor's office have effectively removed the budget for my night on the town.

Thanks to bad knees, I can't dance anyway. And at least three prescriptions are causing drowsiness! I can't even stay awake through dinner at home. O.K., so my cholesterol is lower, but I'm too tired to have a heart attack doing anything, anyway.

I'm sure looking forward to eternal life... but I'm hoping it will be as a 20-year-old!

Thanks for lettin' me share... Amen.

Dear God...
How Do I Look?

I know all of yer children can't look as great as some of 'em do. O.K. I get that. But do I have to look like my mom's Aunt Ethel? As a man, this is rather disconcerting! I'm sure Aunt Ethel isn't happy, either. She has more hair on her chin than I can grow on my whole face! I've heard that "beauty is in the eye of the beholder." That's not in the Bible, is it? There is no accounting for taste. I've seen pictures of natives in foreign lands and what they do to make themselves look more attractive. Like yankin' on their ear lobes or puttin' hockey pucks in their bottom lip, poking holes in their skin tryin' to make something stand out.

Why is it that most of us are not happy with the way you have designed our features? I'm probably not the only potato-head that would like to make a card game outta these discrepancies. I'd rather fold, but I might hang in there if the dealer can give me three new cards. "I'll give you one 'ski slope of a nose' for two 'not-so-droopy eyelids.'" "Didn't you say 'go fish'?"

Have you noticed how much time we, as your creations, spend making "improvements" on your original design? We work it, cut it, paste it, color it, style it, staple it and cover it up. I'm thinking, that "Cover Girl" look on the magazine means she's really hiding everything well.

Now, some of the body image problems might be our own fault, but, frankly, my legs are too short to accommodate this barrel-shaped chest. And my ankles are missing, too. My calves just run down to my feet! I'm told to wear black all the time 'cause it has a slimming effect. Now I just look like the night sky! People are seeing whole constellations on my shirt. Orion's Belt has gotten a lot bigger, too, by the way.

I'm suspicious that you've left me a lot to be desired so that I might work on my personality. It's the only thing that's in good shape these days. I'm lookin' forward to that new "heavenly body" you promised. I hope you don't mind, but I've sketched out a few alterations I'd like to suggest for mine. Unless we're all being fitted with those flowing robes because yer not happy with body images, either.

Thanks for lettin' me share... Amen.

Dear God... Can We Do Away With Mondays?

I know the week has got to start somewhere. But it's taking me a day to remember what I was doing before the weekend. My head isn't really here 'til Tuesday, anyway.

I was thinking we could collect all the Mondays and put 'em in one place on the calendar. Kinda like the opposite of a spring break. Get 'em over with in one giant fell swoop. It would save me a lot of money too, for medications. My prescription for anti-depressants runs out after two weeks. That's only 14 of the 52 Mondays I have to deal with in a year.

There are over a month of Mondays! It just seems a little out of balance when you really look at it. I know nothing gets done on Fridays, either, 'cause I'm already planning for the next two days. But if we could do away with Mondays, we could shorten the waste of time to just one day!

As God, I'm sure you hate to see this kind of waste. I'm just tryin' to be efficient here. Make the most of my time. I know you'd be more pleased with my productivity in a constructive endeavor. I dropped this note in your suggestion box in the lobby of my church, but I wasn't sure you'd see it today 'cause yesterday was Sunday!

Thanks for lettin' me share… Amen.

Dear God... About Hell...

Be honest here, parenting is your way of punishing me for my sins, isn't it? They tell me when you die, your life flashes before your eyes. Well I'm not dead yet, and I'm reliving all the stupidity of my youth via my teenage kids! Is this your way of getting back at me?

I really thought I'd love to play your part as God. But, frankly, getting someone else to conform to the rules and regulations of the universe is just exhausting. I feel like a probation officer. I've learned the hard way what the rules are, but why do I have to explain them to someone else and demonstrate how consequences work?

I was wondering if I could just duplicate your actions at Sodom and Gomorrah—consume them with fire and be done with it. They never learn, they never listen and they remind me too much of me. It's just embarrassing, to say nothing of the extreme inconvenience. I never have pocket money for myself anymore, and nobody puts anything back where it was. I even hide the cookies these days, or I won't get one.

Never in my life have I wanted so much to be a grandfather, where kids only come to visit. There's about ten years of my life I'd like to have move a little faster, please. I now believe there is a real and literal hell. It's where I'd also like to send my kids right now.

Thanks for lettin' me share... Amen.

Dear God... Thanks For The Woman You Gave Me, But...

Yer not gonna take her back, are ya? I lost the first one in a recall. She told me she was made for a "Godly Man," and I just couldn't meet the requirements. I'm not even sure what a Godly man looks like. Probably a lot taller, with fewer defects. But this new lady seems pretty adaptable to the substandard model. You hypnotized her, didn't you? Well, thanks for the help. But I'm still having trouble with the operating procedures.

I personally think yer a little short on instructions in the manual, too. I gotta have illustrations. Women seem to be terribly complicated. And the instructions are too generalized. Startup procedures change almost every day. And sometimes the external switches don't work at all. I've managed to find all the warning lights pretty quickly, though. Alarm bells are going off all the time. She even starts backing up on her own.

She is gorgeous, but the thing is, I'm not sure I'm qualified to do the maintenance all by myself. Her inner workings don't make an ounce of sense to me. I guess you made quite a few improvements on the female model to start with. I don't know how you did that, starting with only a single part from the original male version and adding all the upgrades like you did.

I wondered if you just plain couldn't find another good thing about a man. One rib? You gotta be kidding. So how can you blame us for not being compatible with the new version?

Thanks for lettin' me share… Amen.

Dear God... You Send Angels?

Do you dress up angels in disguise? Make 'em look like really irritating people? In yer book there's this one passage where it speaks of "entertaining angels unaware." Lots of people like to jump on that little quote. But it just makes me a little paranoid. Several people have turned this "angel" idea into decent-selling books. I read that book, *The Shack* by Paul Young, too, where he paints a picture of you showing up at the shack as a large black woman! I haven't seen large black women the same since. Find myself asking them "big picture" questions like: "So what's the future lookin' like for me?" They respond by grabbing their cell phone and dialing 911. First time I asked, I thought maybe they were phoning in a request to angel headquarters to get an answer for me.

I was asked the other day if I was an angel. I was being pretty irritating. "No I'm not an angel," I told 'em. "But yer no miracle worker yourself," I added. So if I ask an "unaware angel" if they are an angel, are they gonna tell me the truth? Angels don't lie do they? Except maybe Lucifer. I heard he had a top position on your angel staff before he got fired. He lost his position to Michael for being, well, irritating, to put it mildly. I heard he took a third of yer angel crew with him, too.

Sounds to me like they have the potential for being unhappy. So maybe angels in disguise are really not your angels! I have noticed a few irritating people who show up rather magically everywhere. I don't see them dying off at all. So I gotta believe they might exist here. I'd just like to know who's side are they on?

Thanks for lettin' me share… Amen.

Dear God...
Is Mother Nature Your Wife?

I don't mean to get too personal here. But every time Mother Nature throws a tantrum we call it an act of YOU! I don't see any mention of you being married. I know the Bible says Jesus has a bride. But you? Nothin'. I guess she could just be your assistant. But you seem to let her do a lot of talking for you. Earthquakes, famines, floods, tidal waves, hurricanes and tornadoes, or is that just her gettin' upset with you 'cause yer married?

I get that. My wife displays a lot of the same behavior! I used to think anger was the opposite of love, but I'm thinking it's actually part of the equation. Yer buddy, Apostle Paul, says it's "better to marry than to burn." I know he was talkin' about lust, but I traded one "burning" for another. Now I'm just being burned... at the stake. I liked the other burning better. All I know is the gloves have come off now that I'm in a relationship. And you seem to endorse the whole relationship thing for better or worse.

I know Mother Nature often says a lot of great things about you, too! Those sunsets, and that night sky where the moon seems bigger than life, seem to bring out the best in her. It's a romantic thought, anyway! She seems really passionate about you. You bring out a full moon, and her tides rise! I'd like my wife to see me the way

Mother Nature sees you! But, lately, it's just the tidal wave and the famine. How do you do that little trick with the full moon again?

Thanks for lettin' me share... Amen.

Dear God...
I'm In Contempt

I'm angry about women generally, mostly the really good-looking ones. There's an over-abundance of 'em. They're just plain distracting. I hate that they can instantly alter my thought process from whatever it was that I was doing a minute ago. To say nothing of the stupid things I've found myself saying to them.

I'm sure they spend an enormous amount of time working on looking that good, just to mess up my day's productivity. And, of course, if I notice too much, they act like I'm some kind of pathetic dog. "You're objectifying women," they tell me. Well, then, maybe you could convince women to stop spending so much time highlighting their... "objects."

I don't need this problem! It makes me look weak and unattractive. It doesn't make the one woman I love too happy with me, either. So I'm supposed to pretend that I am unaffected? Feels like the beginning of the sins of omission. It's the truth nobody can handle about my disposition. So that's why I'm talking to you about it. I don't dare tell anyone else.

So can you be surprised that, in the name of appropriate behavior, I begin to pretend that I'm somehow above the basic laws of nature? I start lying to myself in order to get along with other people. I quietly leave out a little of the truth. And then, of course, you are unhappy with me, too, for being a pathetic liar unwilling to be honest about anything whatsoever.

Excuse me? Some of your favorite guys in Scripture had whole collections of women. And I'm catching hell for even noticing one more than I can have! It's unfair, unreasonable and downright irritating. Go ahead, slap me with another fine for contempt. What's new?

Maybe that's why I lie in the first place. 'Cause the truth always makes you pay. It's just information for other people to use against you.

Thanks for lettin' me share… Amen.

Dear God... Can We Talk?

I'm still tryin' to figure out why it is not good for a man to be alone. I seem to end up that way more often than not. Usually right after a conversation I'm having about the relationship I have. Considering I'm supposed to be someone created to have a relationship, I don't see any natural affinities in that direction. I am talking specifically about the whole man/woman conflict. There seems to be nothing natural about communicating with each other.

I was wondering if there was a residual effect from that whole tower of Babel incident. The woman you gave me doesn't make any sense to me! Words are coming out of her mouth at an alarming rate. I have to take notes! 'Cause I know two days from now there's gonna be a quiz.

She likes to throw out this one line: "What did I just say?" And I sure as hell better not say, "Oh, were you talking that whole time?" I'm tryin' to hear her, really! I've reached a point where I repeat back verbatim, and that seems to suffice. But, so help me here, my comprehension score is hovering around zero.

Fortunately, I do seem to be able to read "body language." There is no doubt there when she is angry. And her body has a way of sayin', "Get out! Get out now! Before there are any injuries!"

"It is better to dwell in the corner of a rooftop than with a brawling woman in a wide house." Well, thank King Solomon for me for that little nugget.

Thanks for lettin' me share… Amen.

Dear God... I'm Driving, And I Can't Stop For Directions

You know how a man hates to stop and ask for directions. Did you install that defect on purpose? I should have stopped a while back. I don't see anything in my life that looks familiar. I read something confusing in your version of the road atlas. "There is a way that seems right to a man, but it ends in destruction." I tried pickin' a way that didn't seem right to me, either, and I got to destruction in half the time. I'm wondering if all roads lead to destruction. It's really not hard to find. I wish you would lay out the map a little more like those mazes in the coloring books at Denny's—you can see the dead ends from the overview.

Mapquest highlights the right road in blue. The maps at the gas station have little green dots to show you the scenic route. But neither of 'em suggest whether yer goin' up hill or down. So is the right path really the "straight and narrow"? Well, you'd think you wouldn't get lost on something like that. If I'm singing, "The Long and Winding Road," does that mean I got off on the wrong exit?

And what about forks? How do I make the right choice here? I've been kind of assuming the right road would be the one less traveled. Probably uphill all the way, and not paved, either. But, hey, maybe I'm the only idiot dumb enough to follow a road that goes nowhere. Maybe there's a reason why nobody takes that road. And have you watched when I've asked more than one person for directions? Here's where the “counsel of many” creates a giant bottleneck.

We got GPS satellite now. This woman’s voice telling me where to go. Sounds really familiar. She warns me, too, and I still get misdirected. I can hear her exasperation: there’s a little pause, and she says, “Recalculating.” Yer voice isn’t as loud as hers, by the way. Maybe you could turn up the volume just a bit. I might be suffering from a hearing loss. I know you gave me a “life map,” but there’s a lot of pages in there. Do I have to read the whole thing? I’d let you drive, but then what control would I have?

Thanks for lettin’ me share… Amen.

Dear God...
Where's The Party?

I read that story about the Prodigal Son. His dad was a little more financially set than I am, I think. I don't have any servants, for one thing. Secondly, I don't have "an inheritance" to give my kids. So when they blow money and then come back to me, I'm not really inclined to throw 'em a party. I gotta make 'em pay it back. I appreciate the thought here in this story, but it's not really fitting my circumstances.

I guess I could get him a "Welcome Home" card. But there's gonna be a list of chores on the back and a few reasonable expectations to meet in order to live here. It doesn't seem to me like that would be a lack of love. It's more a process of teaching that kid some responsibility. I worked hard for the money I gave him. And this is what I get? Downright inappreciative, these kids today. And that disrespectful little… I don't have time for this nonsense. There ain't enough life-time left for me to make up all the money I've sunk into that kid. Feeding him, buying him clothes, paying for college he never finished. He wrecked two of my cars! Remember that? I took your name in vain a couple of times.

I guess I just relate more to the other son in the story. I've been slaving away. So if all he had to do the whole time was ask for a party and dad woulda shelled out, then I guess

I'm asking you. I'd like for you to throw me a big party. Roll the carpet out. Put on a spread. Make it last a whole week or two!

...I don't have to invite my kids, do I?

Thanks for lettin' me share... Amen.

Dear God... Let Me Affirm My "Positivity"

I'm trying to have a "positive" attitude down here. I've always assumed that the word "positive" meant something good, but lately it seems to be a confirmation of bad news. Like when the doctor says, "The results are positive." Now, you'd think that was a good thing.

So yesterday when my financial guru told me, "You need to be more positive," I'm not sure what he meant. Yeah, well today the results are positive that I do not have a positive outlook. You can talk about the glass half full or half empty, but it doesn't change the amount of liquid in the cup. It's a paper cup, too, as I see it. And it has a pencil hole puncture in the bottom.

In the political arena, they talk a lot about putting a "spin" on the truth. In my case, the spin's like this: I'm positive that if my neighbor doesn't do something about his yapping little dog, the future looks promising that I will roast his hide on my back yard barbeque. And I'm positive that if I find another pot-smoking device in the bushes next to my front porch, my outlook is hopeful that the kids next door are going to find their faces on the side of a milk carton. See, I'm being positive here. Hey, I like it! I'm smiling already.

Thanks for lettin' me share… Amen.

Dear God... I've Been Summoned For Worry Duty Again

A smiley-faced sidewalk psychologist told me the other day that 90 percent of the stuff we worry about never happens! So I guess worryin' is pretty effective!

But I really need a break. I'm already holding up most of the universe here. And I got another summons today. Could we spread the worry duty around a bit more? I see a few of your followers not worrying enough. It's usually those flower-lovin' tulip-heads that stopped to smell the roses and fell asleep in the fertilizer. They should be worried. They're making me do all the work. I cannot worry for them; it's cutting in on my own time.

I seem to be stuck in the waiting room of unanswered prayers, staring slack-jawed at a boob tube where some banter-weight is talking about how happy he is, and, for just a nominal fee, I can learn his secret. I'm pretty sure I signed in and took a number at least three game shows ago. But I haven't had my name called yet. My request to be dismissed has been ignored so far. Feels like I'm the one on trial here. When can I get a reprieve?

Thanks for lettin' me share... Amen.

Dear God... Sex Is Getting Out Of Hand!

I get that you had to make sex absolutely compelling in the beginning to insure the survival of the species. But have you looked around lately? We got more population than we can feed, and I'm thinking if you could just cut down the sex drive by maybe half, we might have a better chance of survival here.

Nobody can find the "off switch." We've gotten pretty good at using sex to sell everything these days except condoms. Why doesn't that alarm you? Seems to me, the more people we create in your image, the more work you have to do… more complaining in prayers, too, like what I'm doing here.

I'm just sayin' 'cause yer the only one listening to me. I don't see any effort at self-discipline. And we're turning deciduous trees into stacks of diapers that won't last a week! I don't see killing off the rainforest to keep little Johnny's pee-pee from developing a rash. And what does he do with it in a few years? He starts a whole new generation of little bastards. He doesn't bother with the upkeep and the teaching once they're here, either. Surely, you have the power to stifle the excessive erections; it's taking the blood directly away from the brain, obviously.

Thanks for lettin' me share… Amen.

Dear God...
When Is It Meddling?

I've been tryin' to have "fellowship" with a community of believers like you said to. Suddenly, it has become obvious that I am not lining up with Scripture in one direction or another. You know what I'm talking about here. We've talked about this for a while.

My quiet defiance is getting a little louder, I think. I'm being asked to "step away" from the group because of my sins. Well, I see how I'm not conforming to the desires and will of the greater assembly. But I thought I was working on these issues. Somehow, I've turned into a piñata.

It's taking me longer than I expected to turn my life around; I'm embarrassed about that. They say this is for my own spiritual growth, but this feels like forcing a flower to open.

I heard 'em singing, "Come Just as You Are," in the beginning, but now they don't like what I brought with me. Could I go somewhere else? Is there somewhere else that I belong? I've been thrown out of too many "communities" already.

Thanks for lettin' me share... Amen.

Dear God... I'm Requesting Corrective Lenses

I am having a "vision" problem. I've been "walking by faith" long enough. It feels more like a blindfold. I can't tell if I'm circling the proverbial desert or circling the drain. All I can see is a cloud by day. And that cloud is not moving.

I don't trust your directions… did I write 'em down wrong? Did I leave out a turn somewhere? Yer instruction manual says, "Without a vision, the people cast off restraint." I get that. I don't wanna sacrifice when I can't see the point. But I'm not sure what I should be aiming at in the way of a "vision."

Right now, all I have is a television. I'm about as distracted here as I am in my life on the couch. I'm changing the flippin' channels as soon as I lose interest. It's right where the commercials come in, too. Usually, someone's pitching their own vision for me to join. But, personally, I'd like to have one of my own.

Trouble is, after I finish my projections and assessments about worthwhile stuff to do, I conclude that King Solomon was right: "Everything is meaningless and chasing after the wind."

I have a camera with a telephoto lens so I can get a picture of the mountains without all the telephone poles in the foreground. I wish I had a spiritual version of that. At least let me trade my foggy goggles in on a pair Bifocal Ray Bans. Yeah, with a flip up set of binoculars on 'em.

Thanks for lettin' me share... Amen.

Dear God...
You Know.

I need to talk to you about this whole sexual lust thing. You know what I'm talking about, right? I can barely bring it up in a conversation with anyone without stimulating a little more than the imagination.

My mind is always on fire, usually at the most inconvenient times, like sittin' in church. I can't hear you over the erotic thoughts in my head. I've read the fine print in your contract. I'm tryin' to keep my nose in the good book, but my eyes keep wandering off the page.

It's church, for cryin' out loud! But my dirty little thoughts followed me right in here. I'm singing, "Nearer, My God, to Thee," but it's comin' out with a whole new implication.

"Keep the fire in the fireplace," someone told me once. Trouble is, I got one fireplace and a whole lot of colder rooms up in the house. I appreciate the opportunity to rule my own desires. But your recommended restrictions on sexual release are pretty tight in today's standards.

Frankly, I don't wanna restrict myself when it feels like everybody else is getting to do what they want. Most of the time, it feels like just so much free entertainment.

Last Sunday, the pastor was talking about this new "Heart of Love" campaign. They had passed out buttons for everyone to wear. He gets up and says, “How many of you have your heart on?” For a minute, I thought he was exercising his gift of discernment!

Thanks for lettin’ me share… Amen.

Dear God...
I Don't Want To!

I've been thinking about the whole concept of "delayed gratification." It seems to be getting lost somewhere between "seize the moment" and "missed opportunity."

What's the joy in waiting for stuff? What if it never comes back around? Hey, I can still remember that show *Let's Make a Deal*. I can take the "good stuff" right in front of me, or I can go for what's behind door number three!

Who knows what's back there? Maybe it's a free installation of a burned-out basement, or a year's worth of last year's National Geographic.

With you, sometimes I feel like the dog sitting in position, waiting for his master to drop the biscuit. I really don't wanna wait on your divine delivery here. I want what I want when I want it! And right now, what I don't want is to wait for what I want!

How 'bout if I just go after it now and if it's wrong, get forgiven afterwards. What you see as an exercise in restraint and a building of strength and character, I'm kinda seeing as a waste of perfectly good "redemption."

All the great saints seem to have a redemption "testimony." Maybe I could build on mine a little more. There's very little press coverage for doing the right thing.

In fact, I'm pretty sure nobody notices 'cause everybody's listenin' to Frank Sinatra singing, "I Did It My Way."

Thanks for lettin' me share… Amen.

Dear God... Can We Take A Vote?

It just dawned on me that heaven isn't a democracy, is it. Down here, we'd really like you to be a Republican. I got some friends prayin' for a victory for one presidential candidate. Trouble is, I'm prayin' for the other guy.

When do you step in here? Do you collect all the prayers and go with the majority? I was hoping you might be the swing vote. I always assume that you run eternity much like we run the good ole U.S. of A. After all, this is a "God-fearing" country, they say.

But, with all due respect, you've let some really interesting people into power over the world's history.

I hope it's not a sign of impending punishment here if we made a mistake in choosing. I know of several prayers this month I wished I could recall myself.

I usually vote for who's gonna make my life more comfortable. I'd like good health insurance, by the way. I know I'm asking for the impossible from the government. But maybe you could work a miracle here.

I don't know anyone who is opposed to that one, except maybe the insurance companies. They're pretty comfortable, I think. I hope you're not answering their prayers. I'm pretty sure they're outnumbered on this one.

Thanks for lettin' me share… Amen.

Dear God...
Which Way Do I Pray?

I got a friend who has terminal cancer. You know him. My natural inclination is to pray for his healing. I don't see how you are glorified by a slow, painful death.

Lots of cancer patients have gone unhealed, from where I stand. There must be other purposes in play in all this suffering. I'm sorry, but I'm feeling some resentment towards you for takin' him this way.

I know we who love him are reminded that this life is temporary. But why do you have to drag out the ending of his life? All I can do, in his final weeks, is take care of his dog.

I feel helpless here. Don't know what to say to him or how to pray, really. He's facing something I have no experience with personally. One thing is for sure—there is a different focus for all of us. Our priorities are arranged differently. We've lost the luxury of cynicism. We have no hope without you on this one.

Don't know what direction to pray in. Be with him, I guess, and give us strength to not make it about our loss and our needs.

Thanks for lettin' me share... Amen.

Dear God... I Have A Little Constructive Criticism

I hate to bring this up, but it seems like life is set up in the wrong direction, as I see it. Right when I finally learn how to do stuff, I start losing my physical ability to do it!

I suppose you set that up on purpose so that I must interact with the new kids in the world. The old guy becomes the teacher? I'm having trouble dealing with younger people, they're so stupid. They don't even want to know what I've learned over the years!

The truth is, I'm feeling like what I've learned isn't relevant. The world has changed so much that my experiences seem outdated. At this age, I'm forgetting stuff, too. I was telling a kid the other day about the stuff I used to do. Then I recall, wait, that wasn't even me. I think I might have seen that on TV.

I'm not even sure what my experiences were. Maybe I read that somewhere. My friends are dyin' off, too, so I can't even consult someone who was there. I appreciate that part of your plan, though—no one can really argue with me about what I once knew.

Thanks for lettin' me share... Amen.

Dear God...
Got Anything Bigger?

I appreciate a chance to work with you here, but I don't think I'm really cut out for this quiet, daily routine kind of faithfulness. I was wondering if you had a bigger position for me? I've been with you for some time, and I feel like I've outgrown this position. I'm not really living up to my potential, I don't think.

I guess I'm asking for a promotion. I believe I've done my service here pretty admirably over the years. But my thought is that I should branch out. I could really get the ball rolling if I were given a better position of power and authority. Maybe you have a slot for me with a more official title, to start with. I need something that would look good on a letterhead.

The really important people aren't getting back to me, currently. This anonymous loving and quiet giving to others doesn't appear to be the most effective way of changing the world. I asked a friend if he'd thought about change in his life. He said, "Yeah, I keep it in a jar under the bed." This is what I deal with! I could really be effective if I were working with people who had a higher level of understanding to begin with.

Thanks for lettin' me share… Amen.

Dear God...
I Quit!

O.K., I heard that same message again from a preacher talking about not "stumbling" other people with your behaviors. Frankly, I'm offended by people who are offended so easily! Somebody is offended by everything I say and do.

I'm getting tired of tiptoeing around these people so they can be happy. I've spent a great deal of time trying to convince everyone how perfect I've become since knowing you. You and I both know it's not really true.

The often-offended are gonna find some reason for not having a relationship with you 'cause maybe that's what they really want. O.K., I won't cuss around first-graders and tell 'em there's no Santa Claus, but after that, I am not gonna be codependent anymore.

Hey, nobody's worried about trippin' me up. Offended people make me wanna quit all the time! Personally, I think you might offend them more than I will. So they're gonna blame me for their poor decisions? How cheesy is that?

I'm seeing a danger in making the world completely black and white for the sake of the color-blind. My world has a lot of pastels in it. I didn't invent those colors, either. And somebody is upset about the crayons I'm using. I get that my color spectrum is probably too dark, but I'm not staying inside the lines!

I've painted by numbers before. Not much creativity in

that. That's not what you want, is it? I noted yesterday the shades of gray in the clouds you made. It was spectacular and not like anything I've ever seen before. I want to paint like that. But you just know someone will be irritated 'cause it doesn't look like the sunset they saw yesterday.

Thanks for lettin' me share... Amen.

Dear God...
Mind If I Smoke?

Someone told me, "You won't go to hell for smoking, you'll just smell like you've been there." I know it ain't good for ya. I picked it up in rehab! Along with an obsession for coffee—I drink at least a pot a day. People talk like if I know you real well, I'll just be all shiny all the time. Don't drink, don't cuss, and don't smoke. I don't even like hangin' out with people like that. It's usually fat people telling me how awful it is to smoke! I used to be fat before I started smoking, by the way. Why is it that we all have something we need to hang onto? Trying to trust you and let go of everything else is like trying to get a cat off a curtain.

We can't pass legislation about carrying guns around, but I'll be damned if we can't declare war on the guy who wants to stand away from the rat race for a minute and blow it all off... and flick the ashes, too.

You know, I started smoking as a way of "flicking" people off in the first place. My thinking was, "If a person can't handle this little diversion, they don't wanna know the rest of the story." Now, it's more of a real addiction, I guess, 'cause I'm just not that angry anymore. But Virginia Slim is always willing to stop a minute and help me think through the trouble. The Marlboro Man is usually willing to stand around and talk with ya, too. Non-smokers send you a freaking invoice if you have a conversation with 'em. 'Cause they're running late for their aerobics class.

I know I gotta give this up sometime, or I'll pay through the lungs on the way out to see you. I just wish you had something healthier I could do with the anxiety I have. Maybe that is why some people burn candles and incense and have little rituals with their religion; it helps with the twitchiness. The Catholic Church probably has a whole side business making candles. There are just too many minutes in the day where I'm waiting on you for the next assignment. You saw what the children of Israel did while they were wandering around the wilderness. They started making little idols to worship. Maybe 'cause they couldn't grow anything in the desert. I guess smoking is a sign that I'm still not where I wanna be. But an ashtray is certainly symbolic of where a lot of my dreams went up in smoke.

Thanks for lettin' me share... Amen.

Dear God... What Kind Of Music Do You Like?

I keep hearing the same music at your house. It's the same four chords and seven words. Is everybody but me getting a spiritual buzz off of this? Hey, if yer likin' it, I'll just shut up. But the truth is, I have a different melody and groove in my head than what I'm hearing in church. With all the different music styles, I wondered what you like.

I know you've allowed different denominations based on preferred views theologically. Should there be musical denominations as well? I went to a Church On The Rock, but they were singing country! You seem to be endorsing the guitar-strumming churches these days where the guy singing sounds like he's on Prozac!

It's kind of depressed worship. Is anything that comes out of the heart considered acceptable? 'Cause I would like a real backbeat and some creativity in the lyrics. I imagine something with a challenge to sing. That would feel a little more transcendent to me. But then, nobody's joining me on the chorus.

Is syncopation really of the devil? I read somewhere how much you enjoy fractals. I've seen your creativity in patterns all over the universe. And certainly in all the personalities you've created in people. Do we have to dumb down the music to the lowest common denominator? Do you "inhabit" that as worship?

Thanks for lettin' me share... Amen.

Dear God... You Are Disrupting My Flow!

I've made a pretty good career out of sadness and sarcasm over the years. I really appreciate the blessings lately, but you are messing things up. See, most people down here are truly unhappy and disgruntled about one thing or another. They like to hang out with like minds they can commiserate with. It's how I've made my living for all these years.

Truth is, I've gotten pretty comfortable with my demeanor. I'm used to carrying my own sins and hanging on my own cross. I've felt like a true "survivor" of abuse of every kind. Pain has been my medal of honor. I'm respected 'cause I've been there. Lied to, cheated on, treated like dirt. I've reached the pinnacle of misery!

So I can't take any more happiness this week! I'm losing friends who can't possibly relate. I'm suspected of drug abuse. I'm losing a sense of trust with others, and their confidence in my sanity is at an all-time low. I find myself pretending to be depressed in order to fit in. I feel like such a fake.

I've been talking to you way too much, I think. That might be the problem. I'm not whining out loud as much. A satisfied look is downright suspicious in this day and age. My mental capacity is being challenged. And what do I do with that? I laugh! Which just adds fuel to the fire! Please remove this giddy grin before someone gets hurt.

Thanks for lettin' me share… Amen.

Dear God...
Are You Mad At Me?

I haven't heard much from you in a while. You mad? Things haven't been too exciting last several months, just this daily routine. Where are the miracles? Nobody told me that faithfulness was gonna be this boring. Where's the storyline going?

There have been very little highs or lows recently. I wondered if maybe I crossed one too many boundaries with you. Nothing is going right. At least not the way I want it. I thought we were in this together. Whatever happened to, "Knock and it shall be opened unto you"? Hey. I've knocked and knocked, and the doors are locked. I always gotta jimmy a window to get in to my own plans. And where's the help? I'm doing most of it by myself.

It's kinda hard to lead the charge when no one is behind you. And there's always a sideline quarterback in my face with some smug commentary, "Well, God just isn't blessing your efforts." What I really hate is that maybe he's right, which makes me work that much harder just to show him up! But you ain't sayin' nothin', and I don't see him doing anything at all.

Are you ever passive-aggressive? I'm lookin' back over the Scriptures and over history. You've been pretty emphatic when somebody got yer dander up. All I know is, I'll be "following" you and your will, and the next thing I know, I'm out in front of you.

I'd like to believe this part of my life is a lesson in overcoming adversity. But I'm worried that it's closer to the plagues you allowed in Egypt. Right now I feel like Lord of the Flies!

Thanks for lettin' me share… Amen.

Dear God...
I'm Not In The Mood

I know I don't have to tell you what a day this has been. It would be great if we could have this fantastic connection that would make things feel better, but I'm just not there. I can't summon up a single euphoric thought. I'm just exhausted and a little depressed. I think our dialog together has been pretty one-sided recently, I must say. And to tell you the truth, I'm not getting much out of it. You never say anything, and right when I wish you would... nothing!

I feel ridiculous sometimes tryin' to have a relationship with you. From my perspective you are as difficult a relationship as I have ever had. Mostly 'cause we don't ever do anything together that I want to do. It's always gotta be "your way or the highway." It feels like you don't consider my feelings at all.

I know you're probably distracted with all the work you've got goin' on. But sometimes I think your work is more important to you than me. Why does everything always have to be on your time schedule? I think you discount all the effort I put into this relationship. I give, and I give, and there's not even a, "Thank you," for the little things. Why do I bother? Are you even listening to me? Don't just sit there and act like I'm all crazy!

It takes two to make a relationship work, you know. When do I ever get a break? I feel like I'm doin' all the work here to make things happen.

I would just appreciate a little help on your end. It's the least you could do. Pick up after yourself once in a while. I'm so stupid, enabling you like I always do.

Thanks for lettin' me share… Amen.

Dear God... You And Me Right?

I'm sorry I've been whining a lot! We're still good, aren't we? You and me? I know you're in charge. I get really frustrated 'cause I can't have your job. I'm jealous of your talents, too! I'd love to create something out of nothing. It seems like what I'm tryin' to do down here all the time!

I'm grateful you even listen to me. Nobody else does. It's probably why I keep showin' up for these little one-sided conversations.

I write for a living, but I'm not exactly reaching biblical sales at this point. Probably it's because I contradict your words a lot. I think people resonate with the truth in its purest form best. But you know not everybody's happy with your thoughts, either. I might be at the top of that list myself.

I was thinking about that time up in Canada where I learned how to sail. I had a great little boat. It was really small for the size of the lake, though. And you let the wind die off right when I was in the middle. I just sat there with all of my new-found knowledge and skill. Two hours went by, and I could do nothing until you brought the wind back.

You're not like anyone I know. I mean, I can see character qualities that look like you. I can tell your offspring sometimes 'cause they have your eyes. I've been telling people how you are my father. They don't see the resemblance. That's how I know I'm adopted!

Anyway, thanks for taking me in. I wouldn't have anybody if it weren't for you. And thanks for all the gifts, too, even if I do take them and you for granted.

Thanks for lettin' me share... Amen.

Dear God...
Send Money!

I heard a new, old phrase yesterday: "Jehovah Jirah." I was told it means, "The Lord provides." So… when is that gonna happen? I got bills piling up! I heard a song about you years ago — "He Owns the Cattle on a Thousand Hills" — I was wondering if you wouldn't mind selling off a couple of those heifers and gifting me the money. I'm really falling behind. My faith is doing nothing for my finances.

I always hear your commanders talking about a "faith gift." They are never talking about what they are gonna give me, by the way. I know that platitude: "Give a man a fish, and you'll feed him for a day; teach a man to fish, and you'll feed him for a lifetime."

Lately, the fishing hasn't been too good. So now what? I read from one of those Gideon Bibles in the hotel: "If a child asks for a loaf of bread, will you give him a stone"? Well, I need the bread, in some form of a loan. Everybody wants their money up front. And my debtors aren't too impressed when I tell them to "trust God."

I was at the Bank yesterday trying to acquire some working capital, and they weren't impressed with you as a co-signer, either. I'm currently walking through the "valley of the shadow of debt."

Thanks for lettin' me share… Amen.

Dear God... I Absolutely Love You Sometimes

I don't say it enough because I'm trying to figure out the dilemmas. But I eventually find insights into how your plan works together for good. And it's mostly because of the problems. I see how you keep life interesting. You turn sadness and heartache into euphoric redemptions.

I have feelings I wouldn't have had if not for the fears followed by relief. Things I wouldn't have learned if not for the hardships. My trust in you would not be realized without an awareness of the feelings of mistrust.

Thanks for all of it... and thanks for lettin' me share... Amen.

Dear God... It's An Emergency!

Thanks for seein' me on such short notice. I didn't have the time to fill out the paperwork on this request. It just came up unexpectedly. That "prosperity doctrine" kind of backfired on me. See, I took a few liberties with my own judgment. Actually, I might have taken a liberty from my judgment. But I'm in a serious mess, here. I don't wanna write down the specifics anywhere 'cause it might incriminate me. I don't need any more transcripts for the inquiry. I just need you to fix it!

I can't pay you back right away, either. I promise I'll never do it again. I'll go to church three times a week, sign up for door-to-door evangelism. You can send me to Ubangi as a missionary or something. I was doin' just fine for a while; I even had some Scriptural endorsement about how you wanted me to prosper. I was tryin' not to be that third guy in yer story who buried his master's talents of gold. You know, be the other guy, make it pay off double in half the time. What's gonna happen here, though, is somebody is gonna bury me if you don't step in.

I meant to ask you for wisdom early on, but I really had to move on this opportunity. I was just "seizing the moment." Now I'm having a "seizure salad" before I start eatin' crow. For that matter, this might be more like my "last supper" before they hang me on a cross. Jesus died for my sins right? So didn't he pay for this already? These people aren't quite as forgiving as Jesus. I'm wondering if he could bust me out of jail later this year.

Thanks for lettin' me share… Amen.

Dear God...
Can I Pay?

Listen, I appreciate what you've done for me, but the one thing I hate more than being needy is being indebted to someone. It just hangs over my head like an unfinished homework assignment. In this case, I believe that what your son, Jesus, did for me on the cross—pickin' up the tab on all my sins is the way I've been told—leaves me with a sense of enormous debt in the way of gratitude. A gratitude that comes with a compounded interest that is so high, the payoff amount doubles with every statement!

I'm horrified! Of course, I'm paying only the minimum daily requirements allowed by law. I've tried to be really good and not screw up because, frankly, to simply "believe and receive" this offering as a true gift doesn't seem to cut it with those who are expecting way more in the way of personal behavior.

"Expected gratitude" has a way of feeling a little like a personal loan that can't be paid off in this lifetime. I've been told I have to leave everything to you in my will! You've seen my will, right? I keep changing it, for one thing. I can't imagine what you'd want with anything that I have, frankly. And to make matters worse, I was told that everything I have, I received from you to begin with. So let me get this straight, you want me to give it back?

I'm pretty sure that I am the guy in that parable who buried his "talents." Only, I'm not even sure where I might have dug that hole!

Thanks for lettin' me share… Amen.

Dear God... What's The Deadline Again?

I've been going to more funerals than weddings lately. I was at a funeral the other day, and I started thinking about that cartoon where a doomsday prophet is holding a sign that says, "The end is near." Then he gets run over by a truck! I'm sure you heard that one first. According to you there is no end. It reads more like a reconfiguration or a transformation, maybe. But the fear of dying sure feels like the end of the world as I know it.

So the Doomsday dude is partially right. It's just one person at a time. I'm more than a little nervous about the whole reality of dying. Like Woody Allen said, "It's not that I'm afraid of dying... I just don't want to be there when it happens." So I guess I can't count on Woody to be my proxy, either.

I probably wouldn't spend as much time talking to you, except that I know that black hole is coming. It's worse than a deadline for a book report in high school. I'm starting to see younger kids, now, more as my "replacements." One of them is gonna start filling in for me. Take my job, my house too. They'll probably sell my car, though, 'cause it has as many miles on it as I do.

People who've had near-death experiences tell stories of how they've seen a light to walk towards. I'm just worried about whether I need to pay my portion of the electric bill! I'm countin' on Jesus' version of "affirmative action" for the spiritually impaired. I got an official letter of intent that everybody says is your handwriting. There are a handful of promises here, but I don't have anything to compare your signature to. Please get back to me with a form of reference when you can.

Thanks for lettin' me share… Amen.

Dear God... Please Make It Stop!

It's me again. I'm having these anxiety attacks! All my responsibilities are ganging up on my brain and beating the living crap out of it. I'm starting to vibrate uncontrollably. I thought it might be too much coffee in the morning, but that sits in my stomach.

What I'm feeling is a fifty-pound sack of flour on my chest. The doctor says I'm stressed. And he charged me eighty bucks for that information, by the way, and no prescription! "You need to relax," he tells me. Easy for him to say, he just made eighty bucks in five minutes! And he didn't have to sign in and wait two hours to get that little piece of information.

It's really not my responsibilities that are freaking me out, though. It's the stuff I don't have any control over. That's your department, isn't it? That stuff is screwing up my ability to handle my response!

Can you send me some version of reinforcements? So, what is with Chuck Norris getting all those mad skills? I saw a poster listing all of his abilities to kick the crap out of everything. Was I at the back of the line when those skills were being handed out? Maybe you could "chuck" him over to my house 'cause I'm having a little trouble making good things happen.

I wonder if giving every man a free will was really a good decision on your part. I remember that little statement I heard: "If God can do anything, can he make a rock so big that he can't pick it up?" Maybe that's a clever conundrum. But right now that rock is sittin' on my chest.

Thanks for lettin' me share… Amen.

Dear God...
It's The Old "Whineskin"

I noticed that Jesus died at 33! It was my understanding that he experienced everything a man has to deal with so he could understand our plight. Well here's one thing I think he might have missed, 'cause he didn't live long enough. It's the part where your best years are a decade behind you. Seems to me, he went out at the top of his game, so to speak.

I, on the other hand, am approaching the pinnacle of my decline. I can't imagine Jesus at my age, or even older, sitting on the porch of the retirement home talking about that time he turned water into wine. That was a big hit, I'm sure. Especially 'cause it involved free drinks for everybody!

There was probably a "Water Into Wine" tour that followed. But the next miracle wasn't as well-received. People started talking about "back in the day." The next "Messiah" was already getting more press coverage, too. "Jesus is Old School" was being tossed around in the Jerusalem Post.

I know he lost some popularity, but it didn't seem to last too long. After a three-year career, it reads like he went out in a hail of gunfire, a big finish. Not much time to sit around and wonder if his life was effective. I don't see a point where he had to think about another line of work, either, or watch his friends start dying off. Maybe he had an assurance from you that I'm not feeling.

I'm struggling just to stay busy these days. I can't work miracles, by the way, never could. I gotta tell you, I'm not excited about the concept of eternal life if there ain't something purposeful to do. I hear we're just gonna stand around singing praise music the whole time. I don't like praise music down here already! No offense. The songs don't feel very inspired. Mostly 'cause they don't sound like the music we used to do back in the day. Let's see, that was thirty-five years ago. Wow, the songs I like are older than Jesus. With all due respect, I don't think you've ever heard someone say to you, "Hey didn't you used to be somebody?" Maybe that's why we like wine so much... 'cause at least wine improves with age!

Thanks for lettin' me share... Amen.

Dear God...
Who's Bob Eppu?

When I was real young, I heard a lot of conversations about "speaking in tongues." I never really got the point of not making sense verbally. I got enough people speaking to me now in regular English all at the same time, and I don't even know what they're saying! "Speaking in tongues" is supposed to be some kind of empowering experience that I never quite realized.

I thought you were not the "author of confusion." Do you get the whole speaking in tongues thing? Was that just a one-time happening in the book of Acts? Some circles are trying to recreate that event. I don't see the empowerment from it, though.

The closest I ever got to speaking in tongues is that point where I'm so angry or tired that all my words run together—not very empowering, by the way. It can be funny, though. I remember finishing a concert once, after a long series on tour with my old band, where the drummer, upon leaving the stage, tried to say, "Good night! God Bless You!" It came out, as he screamed into the microphone, "Bah Bep Pooh!"

See, even you are laughing at this, right? Who's Bob Eppu? And why are they paging him to the stage? Maybe he left his lights on in the parking lot. There was a little moment of amused confusion, where everybody paused to consider the ramifications. "BAH BEP POOH"? It was as clear and concise as anything we screamed over the mic all night. It was recited regularly from that point forward as a kind of mantra to our own confusion on the road. "Bob" became our imaginary friend. And it gave us the one standout moment in a blur of cities and concerts that year.

Maybe I'm starting to understand how you might add power to what appears to be complete nonsense and make a highlight out of it! Cool then... let the tongues begin.

Thanks for lettin' me share... Amen.

Dear God...
About Last Night

Should I be apologizing to you for stuff you knew I was gonna do before I did it? Yeah, I was mostly faking it last night. I just wanted people to think you and I were really tight. I was letting people assume that we're getting along just fine. It seems a little redundant to admit it to you, though. How does this work in our relationship? I'm assuming you'd just like to hear me say, "I'm sorry, please forgive me," and mean it. But it's a little embarrassing that I can't hide my motives or intentions or even color the implications just a little. You already know that I'm mostly interested in you for what you can do for me. Besides, what can I give the GOD who has everything?

I got a support group where they keep saying, "Fake it 'til you make it." It was always pretty iffy-sounding. But with other relationships, I have the opportunity to say something and then kind of fill in the right behaviors eventually. Or maybe it was the other way around: do something and let the convictions come later. See, I'm not sure what part I was supposed to fake now. I think I'm currently faking both sides!

Honestly, I'm really not all that sorry about my behavior! I behave like I do because I get something out of it that I enjoy. I just don't like the outcome in the long run sometimes. Right now, I am sorry, though. I'm sorry that I'm not very sorry. I'm sorry that you aren't very happy with me. I'm sorry that I don't have a decent attitude. Sorry that I have to fake any of it.

Thanks for lettin' me share… Amen.

Dear God...
What The...?

I got yer email, via a well-meaning friend. They forwarded some notes to me from you about not using swear words. I call it my "Golf Language." Are you that uncomfortable with the nonsense words people use? Or is that just shaking my friend's comfort level with my lack of sanity. The implications of words seem to change rapidly these days, what with the information superhighway. But cuss words? They've been around forever! It's mostly the same six or seven words. Yeah, maybe it's because they're effective in expressing displeasure and frustration.

I studied a word in the Bible once. O.K., somebody told me about it. The word was "naughty." Back in the day, that was an awful thing to say, but it got used so much that nobody is offended by it anymore. I remember when to say that something "really sucks" was grounds for two bars of soap from my mama. And my grandfather used to whup me for saying "crap."

I can hold words in to be polite. Bite my lip, I guess. But soap in the mouth made me wanna cuss that much more—I was still cussin' in my head. O.K., so the "F-Bomb" is really vulgar. And asking you to damn something to hell might be overstating my authority. It's definitely not a submissive attitude; I get that. My friend always says, "I don't mind you saying that you're sick, but you don't have to throw up on my coffee table to prove it."

Have you ever thrown up? It's not something I wanted to do, either. It's rather involuntary; I can't always make it to the toilet. And by the way, there is a toilet for that stuff, right? I find a lot of people in there throwing up.

If the whole thing is really about using words "in vain," I don't think it applies to cuss words, because they feel pretty effective to me. People who don't like cuss words have their own, though. I call it "near cussing": a verbal version of "near beer!" My dad always used to say, "Well, shoot." What's that? Or how about, "That's a lot of horse feathers." Apparently, "Dad blast it!" was O.K. for my grandfather 'cause that was his word. The preacher's wife would always say, "Oh, for the love of God."

O.K., so "for cryin' out loud"… I'll try to watch my language.

Thanks for lettin' me share… Amen.

Dear God... Talk To My Mother?

I talked to my mom like you told me to. You sound like my earthly father, when I ask him about direction: "I don't know, talk to your mother." Well, Mom's been planning her funeral again, doesn't wanna be a burden to anyone. She's been doin' this for about ten years now.

She said she got a great deal on a pre-owned casket. How does that happen? Anyway, she wants everybody to "celebrate" her life, make it a festive occasion. I hear that a lot at funerals. "They woulda wanted us to be happy," and, "Remember the good times." Are these people in denial?

I gotta say, that's not me. I would like some weeping and gnashing of teeth, please, at my funeral. I want folks to see what they're gonna miss when I'm gone. They're not gonna have me to kick around anymore! I'm worried, though, that nobody's gonna show up. Except maybe all the people I owe money to. As a singer, I already know how hard it is to get people to turn out for anything when yer still alive! You gotta tell 'em three times. Give 'em free tickets and a backstage pass. Promise to be done by nine.

My mama already has invitations printed out for her little gathering. She's pickin' out the music, too. "How come you've never written a song for me?" she says. "Here's my epitaph, maybe you can put that to music." She was also pretty emphatic that she does not want to be burned. Doesn't like the idea, no matter how dead she might be. Now she's talking about having a "green" funeral. It's cheaper, and the coffin is biodegradable. "I don't want anybody digging me up when I don't have time to do my hair first." "I'll be in the same dress I was wearing last year," she says, "what will people think?" "I don't know, Mom," I told her, "at that point, I don't see why you would care."

Don't forget to tell her that her outfit looks nice when you see her. But don't take her for another twenty years. I'm really loving these little conversations!

Thanks for lettin' me share... Amen

Dear God...
Can I Get Extra Credit?

I was looking back over the transcripts of my emails to you yesterday. I sound like a cranky old man! Is that who I am now? I've had my disappointments with the way things have turned out. It wasn't the way I pictured it, that's for sure. I have some serious regrets even now. I don't know why we all worry about the story we leave behind when we're gone. Nobody's gonna read it. But I know I'm not the only one who's losing sleep over how my life will be perceived after the wake.

I'd like a better grade than I know I'm gonna get. Do you think I could work on some extra credit? Raise my standings overall? I'm not really sure what you've got planned in heaven, but if you are expecting us to live purposefully down here, there's gotta be a reason. I'm thinking there's gonna be a pecking order up there. I just know I'm gonna have a cleaning job behind the throne for eternity because my GPA wasn't high enough for a good position.

Hopefully, you'll be grading on the curve. But, then, I'm worried you might be calling witnesses on judgment day. My life could hang in the balance, based on who's gonna take the stand. Did you get a chance to look over my list of witnesses that I'd like to have excluded? There are several people that come to mind that I feel are unfairly biased!

I have my own version of that children's bedtime

prayer: "Now I lay me down to sleep, my best intentions, hope you'll see. If I should die before I wake, don't give my Ex the eulogy!"

Thanks for lettin' me share… Amen.

Dear God...
I'm Not Fitting In

I keep seeing these bumper stickers that say, "Not of this world." I think it's a reference to what you said about becoming new creatures in Christ. No offense, but I always think of the movie *Creature from the Black Lagoon*. That, to me, is what is not of this world.

I've been hangin' around yer people for some time. The longer I look around, the more I feel like I still don't belong even with those who don't belong. I think I'm a defective "creature." And I'm not really new, either.

When do I start looking like the rest of your new creatures? Right about the time my friends say they can see a change in me, I revert back to the same creature from the swamp I came out of. Actually, I feel more like "brundle-fly" from the movie *The Fly*, where the mad scientist transports himself from one chamber to a new one and ends up as half-man, half-fly. Now there's a creature for ya.

Do we really change? I can mimic the behaviors of other new creatures when I really work at it. But, hey, if I can see the self-righteousness, I'm sure everyone else can, too. I keep hearing about this miraculous transformation. Like in the Book of Acts where these people are all hangin' out one night and suddenly they start acting different and "those around all marveled." I'm not seeing that. What I'm seeing is this hideous half-man, half-beast. Nobody is marveling here. Mostly, they're just rolling their eyes. There's no doubt there are some really interesting creatures runnin' around this planet. It's a regular costume party!

I'm thinking that maybe I'm just unhappy 'cause my "new creature" doesn't look original.

Thanks for lettin' me share... Amen.

Dear God... Thank You, And Please Forgive Me

Let me just say, I didn't mean all that stuff I said to you yesterday! I was "under the influence"... of mistrust! I was getting nervous. I know I work for you, but I hadn't heard from you in a while. I was beginning to think my application wasn't goin' through. I'm sorry I still don't trust you with my finances after all this time. I know my appraisal came in lower than you might have wanted. I'm aware, too, that I don't qualify for much credit. Thanks for covering my shortfall again. I got the check today. I'm sorry about wasting two whole weeks worrying. I couldn't see how you were gonna help.

If you hadn't stepped in with that miracle like you did, I'd probably have had to file for bankruptcy. But can we just keep this between ourselves? If my associates knew how I'm just hangin' on by a wing and a prayer, I think my credibility could be ruined. They really like confidence in their cohorts. If you don't mind, I'd like them to believe that I pulled this out all by myself.

Once I'm really on top of the business, I'll be happy to point out your divine intervention. I did point out, however, that they should trust you more with their lives, though. So I didn't leave you completely out of the picture or anything. It's just that I don't wanna sound too religious. I still need their confidence in me. See, if they actually knew what you were capable of doing for them, I, as the middle-man, might be cut completely out of the deal!

Thanks for lettin' me share... Amen.

Dear God... So What's Wrong With The Dark?

You remember me being scared of the dark, right? Well, now, that's my favorite part of the day. It's cooler in the summer. And it's the only time I can sleep. What I'm really afraid of these days is out in broad daylight. It's the realities that I can see headed right for me that put the fear of you in me.

Broad daylight is when the postman comes too, like Santa Claus, only he's bringing a sack full of invoices. Yeah, great, come rain or shine that mail always gets through. I'd like to escape under cover of darkness. But darkness seems to get a bad rap in religious circles.

They turned the lights up in the restaurant last night. Man, you could see how ugly the room really was and how filthy, too. Now, I don't mind candlelight. 'Cause there's no electric bill attached. And it's romantic!

I look younger and healthier in a dim light. And you can't see the marinara sauce that I spilled on my shirt. So what can I say? I love darkness rather than light. I think you said that, too, at some point about all men. But I got the impression that you weren't happy about it. The moon shines brightest on a dark night, and I can stare at it for as long as I want without going blind.

I guess I don't mind the light, it's just the intensity of the bulb. It can get pretty hot, too. I start sweatin' a lot. I get the feeling I'm being interrogated! My fears are coming at me at light-speed, by the way. I can only handle the scrutiny in the light of a 40-watt bulb.

Thanks for lettin' me share... Amen.

Dear God... I'm In The Lost And Found

That guy that wrote the lyrics to "Amazing Grace" said he only got lost once! But now he's found. Well, how nice for him. His song was the biggest hit ever written, too. I think he could afford a GPS on the residuals. Do you actually lose track of people? And then find 'em like in that sheep story? Leave the 99 and go look for the one? Should I yell "polo"? 'Cause if yer looking for me, I've been right here all along.

Someone told me I'm not lost, I'm just extremely confused all the time. Is there a difference? I don't recognize the surroundings I'm in every other day. I'm told to "trust you" and "walk by faith." It still feels like I'm lost, though. And you ain't sayin' much, either. No offense, but I don't think you know how that feels to live daily with a sense of uncertainty and impending doom. "You lead me beside the still water"? I feel like I gotta strain a pound of mud to get an ounce of pure drinking water. I'm afraid there's more than one sheep missing, too, and I'm way down the list for rescue.

In the mean time, I'm out here in the thicket, bleating to death. I'm knee deep in sheep dip. And that dog is just driving me nuts. I've tried to stay in the flock, but all I ever see is another sheep's backside. Sometimes knowing that you know where we're going isn't really helping me.

I've been through more than one "valley of the shadow of death" now, too. When do we get to "lie down in green pastures" again? Is that before or after I've been completely "fleeced"?

Thanks for lettin' me share… Amen.

Dear God...
I Gotta Go To Work

I read a quote from Jesus yesterday. Thanks for printing it in red. He was saying I shouldn't store up treasure on earth 'cause it rots and people break in and steal it. We don't talk about "treasure" anymore, by the way, except in the *Pirates of the Caribbean* movies, where all the booty is piled up in a cave somewhere. We don't "store up" treasure these days... we build equity! So far it's not much of a stockpile, either.

Should I not have a "portfolio"? Most of my money is on paper. I'm really short on "liquidity." He mentioned the possibility of moths and rust corrupting it all. Sounds like clothes and cars might not be the best investment. It figures, I was hoping to get a new car soon. My truck is starting to rust. Is there a difference between "wealth and treasure"? I recall something the great moral philosopher Chris Rock said in one of his sermons: "there's a difference between a rich [dude] and a wealthy [dude]... A rich [dude] buys 21-inch rims for his Escalade" and "a wealthy [dude] provides jobs for other [dudes] and takes care of his family." I'd love to be both! But you never hear the two words together.

At what point does my bank account qualify for a "storing up of treasure"? I'm thinking yer against Jet Skis and motorcycles. Sounds like you don't want me to have any fun while I'm down here. I'm afraid if I really want something good, yer gonna make sure I don't get it 'cause it's selfish. Those 21-inch rims would look good on my truck, too. But providing for my family? Where do I draw that line? My kids have better cars than I do. They expect cell phones, designer clothes and name-brand shoes. They ain't gettin' the fact that I gotta go to work while they're sittin on the couch watching *Pirates of the Caribbean*. I think I might have something stored up, though. A desire to kick a little booty!

Thanks for lettin' me share... Amen.

Dear God... I Need A "Mulligan"

Can I get a 'do over'? Again? I've kinda blown that good first impression. I haven't exactly put my best foot forward with you. It keeps ending up in my mouth. I'd like to take back everything I've ever said to you (except maybe that request for a new motorcycle). I haven't ever seen the bigger picture, I don't think. But maybe, for the first time, I might be aware of that fact.

I'm tired of makin' mistakes down here. I've perfected the art of poor decisions. Apologies have no meaning if nothing changes. So where do you want me to start today? Can I get a work release over jail time? I know what I deserve, but I've heard you are merciful. I'm assuming I'm on probation. Honestly, I've been trying to be you. I don't think that's what you meant when you said to be Christ-like. But maybe you could bring me back from the dead, too.

I've been irritated with most of your friends, discounting everybody. Blaming my circumstances on their decisions, but I thought I balanced that out 'cause I don't like any of your enemies, either. I've blamed them, too. I've blamed everything on everybody. The thing is, I'm making a huge mess out of everything. Maybe you could show me how to rebuild. We'll probably have to tear down everything I've done so far. It didn't seem like a house of cards when I started. But all I can see blowin' around now is coming down in spades!

Thanks for lettin' me share... Amen.

Dear God... What Can I Say?

I read a Saddleback sermon yesterday from Pastor Rick Warren. He's a millionaire 'cause he wrote that book about purpose. All the while his wife is losing her battle with cancer right now. You haven't seen fit to heal her. But I think you've been to their house a lot. He said he sees the world as a preparation for a real eternal life. And circumstances, good and bad at the same time, are like two rails of the same track, designed to take us across the proving ground of life on earth. That's heady stuff to believe!

Are we in boot camp? Is life a matter of practicing for another world? Or are we floating through life aimlessly, here to live in the moment? Forrest Gump says, "I think it's a little of both." I don't necessarily wanna pick my beliefs based on what makes me feel better. I don't think the truth cares how I feel. But believers in this arena seem to have a better attitude all around than, say, a Vegan who lives on lettuce and thinks that is all there is.

What I choose to believe has a profound impact on how I react to my trouble, though. Subconsciously, I've always seen heaven as some kind of giant retirement home where I sit on the front porch in a rocking chair and look down on the people who still have a life. Then again I imagine a recreational resort of sorts in my fantasy life.

Jesus says, in essence, "I go to be with my father." Sounds like he's moving back in with his folks. I'm not sure I would like that.

But I choose to believe the best of you and your plan, whether I know any of it or not. I have walked through life here with believers and non-believers over the years (being a little of both myself). What can I say, I think yer holding all the cards. It's a better hand than I have, I'm sure of that. So I'm gonna fold here. Let you take the whole pot. If Rick is right, I would think the plan for eternity involves a genuine community and harmonious relationships with other souls. Naturally, it's the one thing I've not been very good at. I miss my grandmother, by the way. I'd like to change the last things I said to so many friends and family before they left. But, then, I still don't know what I'd say.

I'm feeling a deeper connection to others somewhere beyond any words. Like when I sit on the back porch with my wife every morning for coffee, watching you bring up the stage lights on the heavens. I can't recall a single thing we say. But there is a satisfied feeling in knowing she's there! I feel better, too, knowing you are there. I guess I'm so frustrated with what you are not telling me that I miss the things you whisper to me everyday. I hope this life isn't just a quiz for the final exam. It seems a little more precious than that. And I like what I feel when I see things from your perspective, even if you are not saying anything at all.

I guess I'd like to say something to you that I've said to the woman I love: "Thanks for being so comfortable with me!"

And thanks for letting me share.... Amen

In memory of

Erica Leanne Forney

August 25, 1999 – November 27, 2008

Self Portrait by Erica

Dear God... About That Moment Of Silence...

My cousin's nine-year-old daughter was struck by a distracted driver and killed. I'm assuming you were there when it happened. I'd ask you why you take little girls, but you've ignored my question before. Maybe it would take too long to explain. But from here it feels like yer pickin' flowers before they've had a chance to bloom. Forgive me for not understanding this. But she was a cherub. She lit up a room wherever she went. The world seems to be a darker place when you remove lights like her.

We both know you could have prevented it if you wanted to. But you didn't. I know that there is an appointed time for all of us with eternity. I just wish you could have scheduled her appointment a little farther down the road. We could discuss the ramifications of the free will that you've gifted everyone, and how it impacts all of us. But that doesn't bring anyone back from the dead.

I'm nearly speechless here. I'm filled with a wild mixture of love and pain, resentment and sadness, and one giant question mark about your plans. Right away I feel responsible to speak for you about why you allow this kind of tragedy. But even an accurate answer would not change the aching of hearts broken. And seeing a nine year old lying in a coffin will never look right to me.

Personally, I can see how you move most of us along as a direct result of the current pain we're in. Nothing seems to change without the pain of loss. It's the only way we overcome our fears of changing the way things are. I pray her sacrifice is not wasted. That what needs to change in our lives here will be brought to pass. And I pray that children lost will speak to us from their shortened lives that we are responsible to love those we love deeply — with all the immediacy that this moment brings.

A friend of yours told me there's a difference between endurance and perseverance. The first is a matter of toleration, while the second is a real pursuit, a moving forward in the belief that "love" will always win, truth will overcome, and darkness will dissipate. I'm picking what's behind door number two in this case.

Take care of Erica for us, give her some hugs and kisses, too. Let us rest in the pleasure of knowing that she is in your arms, safe and secure from all alarm.

And give us the strength to live fearlessly because we knew her to live that way. Until we meet again, Erica, we're leaving a light on for you down here!

Thanks for letting me share… Amen.

Erica Leanne Forney

"Our Sunshine"

Aug. 25, 1999 – Nov. 27, 2008

Erica was an amazing little girl who loved spending time with her family and friends. She was inseparable from her sisters, and she loved animals. She was a prolific and aspiring artist. Erica loved nature, archeology, rocks, and science. She was a natural comedian whose contagious happiness always brought life and joy into the room. Erica loved her church, and she loved God. Everyone who met her fell in love with her instantly.

A few days before Thanksgiving in 2008, Erica was struck on her way home from school within sight of her house by a distracted driver who was reportedly using a cell phone.

A portion of the proceeds of this book will be donated to FocusDriven, an advocacy group for victims of motor vehicle crashes involving drivers using cell phones. FocusDriven helps victims and their families share their experiences in a healing manner that promotes safety and educates others about the tragic outcomes that can result from driving while using a cell phone.

For more information or to get involved, contact:

FocusDriven
P.O. Box 2262, Grapevine, TX 76099

Email info@focusdriven.org | **Phone** 630.775.2405

www.focusdriven.org

About Bryan Duncan

After 40 years of writing and singing music in every possible configuration of Christian Church, this author remains a pragmatic believer in a truly personal relationship with a Real God and the fundamentals of the Bible. "Most of the answers to my prayers have come in the form of a change in my own perspective," he laughs. Here, Bryan offered us his sincere and sarcastic versions of the one-sided conversations he has had with God as he understands him.

Conversation w/ God

Neale Donald

Walsh

---

1 202. 489 6978 Kimmy

tone

CONVERSAYTION w/ God

Neale DONALD
WALSH

1
2
3

---

1 702 489 6978 Kimmy
Hone